My Healing Journey

DARLA FISHER-ODJIG

A Walk in Two Worlds

Duel Identity: A collection of First Nations Art &
Poetry as seen through the eyes of a trauma
survivor

1987
DARLA FISHER-ODJIG POETRY & ART
(An anthology of First Nations Poetry & Art)
1986 Old Woman Story (Intergenerational trauma) *Extreme Opposites (I Walk with a hard shoe on one foot and a moccasin on the other)*

Rivers flow for a reason; bridges are built for a cause. The river flows as directed by nature and her many lines of a ravaged face are evident concerning her structure and environment. We have the choice as to whether we want to go with the flow or build that bridge toward a cause that allows us the control of our own destination.

In this book of poetry and pros I hope to touch the hearts of those who may not understand the long term affects of trauma. There are many treatments for depression, drugs, therapy and whatever else helps to dull those pains of the voices long ago instilled by generations of struggle. I feel that the best medicine is to listen and hear that we are not alone and we can live outside our nightmares within.

These poems will show the many emotions and feelings brought about by those fears and nurtured by the "Seven Grandfathers" as applied toward a better understanding of a balanced value system within. The holistic view of mind, body heart and spirit.

The yearning to be accepted and understood as a resilient and strong person like that of the buffalo.

I have a cause and that being to reach out and teach through my pain, through a humbling that is clear to acknowledge "I am no different from you and you from me" therefore we are the same.

7th. World Aboriginal Image Maker

Vision: the belief that symbology will be a huge part of the art. That all may project a uniqueness of their Indianess through this. We promote the essence of our culture through the educating of our ceremonies & visions through symbols. The sharing through symbology/pictorial imaging precipitates a phenomenon of altruism and healing. Guidance through mind, heart, body and spirit is essential to envisioning a holistic sense of self. In reference to *Creative Extraction,* expression toward the enhancing of emotion and identification of authentic values and feelings enable release and validation. Building of inner strength and outer relationships are important to communicating who we are. Reflecting on shadow imaging and of internal elements will allow for visioning and creative connectedness. Our *Community* includes the participating of connecting with the public through the art and its symbolic representation regarding the intergenerational affect as illustrated by symbolic historical referencing and recording. The developing of inner creativity through outer expression allows a sense of identity and connecting of 2 worlds within. Integrating Aboriginal artistic mastery with Western/European mastery as a recognized fine artistry brings a unified and elegant fusion of a unique vision of true Canadian Fine Art.

FISHER-ODJIG

DARLA FISHER-ODJIG POETRY & ART

D Fisher-Odjig
CAREER SYNOPSIS
Group Exhibitions. Solo Exhibitions
Collections. Commissions Illustrations
& Publications

GROUP EXHIBITION

1982 Queen Elizabeth Building
CNE Toronto. ON
Dalhousie University, Ilalifax
MacDonald Hotel Edmonton
Mississauga Meinnes-Nixon Gallery
Mississauga, ON
Air Canada, Sault Ste. Marie, ON
Sault Ste. Marie Art Gallery, Sault Ste.
Marie, ON
1983 Holiday Inn, Toronto, ON
University of Kitchener, Kitchener, ON
University of Guelph, Guelph, ON
Festival of Arts, Brantford, ON
Westin Hotel Hungers End, Toronto, ON
Sheraton Northwood Hotel Ft.
McMurray, Alberta
Library, Ft. McMurray, Alberta
McDonald Island Trades Fair, Ft. Mc
Murray, Alberta
O.M.N.S.I.A Conference, White
River, ON
1984 Native Canadian Centre
(Ontario Native Artists) by Helen Wilson
Spadina Ave. Toronto, ON
1988-89 Nimkis Gallery, Toronto, ON
1993 Native Canadian Center,
Toronto, ON., CA
1994 Touch The Earth Gallery,
London, ON., CA Sept. 29-Oct. 9
1996 MIZIWEBIIK Aboriginal
Employment, Toronto, ON., CA
1997 Artemis Gallery, Parry Sound,
ON., CA
Festival of Sound

1998 Sky Dome Pow Wow, Toronto,
ON., CA
A.N.D.V.P.
2000 Two Woman Show, Woolfits
Gallery, ON., CA. Oct. 1-29/2009
2001 Neekawnisidok – (All Our
Relations)
Toronto, ON, CA, City Hall (Tundra)
A.N.D.V.P. Association For Native
Development In The Performing &
Visual Arts, ON., CA
2002 Two Woman Show, (Sweet
Medicine Woman) Acme Gallery,
Toronto, ON., CA
2003 Tundra Showing of Native
Aboriginal Art Festival, Toronto, ON, CA
2004 Group Showing Streetsville
Gallery, Aboriginal Treasure,
Mississauga, ON., CA
2006 Aboriginal Treasures Exhibit,
Mississauga, ON., CA, Streetsville
Gallery
2007 FASM, 10th. Anniversary
Celebration, Milton, ON., CA,
1997-2007
2008 FASM, From Heart to Hand,
Milton, ON., CA
2008 Streetfest Arts Festival, Streetsville
Gallery, Streetsville, ON., CA

SOLO EXHIBITION

1986 Ontario North Now, Artists of the
Week, exhibition Place, Toronto, ON
1987 Ontario North Now, Artists of the
Week, exhibition Place, Toronto, ON
1991 Ontario North Now, Artists of the
Week, exhibition Place, Toronto, ON
1988-89 Nimkis Gallery, Toronto, ON
1993 Native Canadian Center,
Toronto, ON
1993 Touch The Earth Gallery,
London, ON

ILLUSTRATION & PUBLICATIONS

1995 Book Steel My Rage, Poetry & Art
Douglas & McIntyre, Joel Maki editor,
Toronto, ON, Na-Me-Rez (Native
Men's Residence)
1995 Book Cover In A Vast Dreaming Art
and Poetry, Native Women In The Arts,
1996 Book Art & Poetry, Let the Drum
Be Your Heart, Douglas & McIntyre,
Warrior Cry, artwork & poetry
New Native Voices, Joel Maki,
Toronto, Ontario
Urban Mozaik Magazine 1997
– Article on D. Fisher Odjig,
SPIRITUALITY BELONGING
By Jennifer Lambert, Toronto, ON, CA
1998 Illustrations Art for Native Women
In The Arts, Women's Free Press
--- Diary Day Calendar, Toronto,
Ontario,
Magazine Aboriginal Voices, Article on
Daphne Odjig, *Notification of
recognition* to D. Fisher Odjig by
Daphne Odjig.
Published book on art and poetry, 2009
grant from the Ontario Arts Council.
"My Healing Journey, A Walk in Two
Worlds." As Seen Through the Eyes of a
Trauma Survivor ."

AWARDS

1995 Indian and Northern Affairs
Museum of Man, Ottawa ON,
Canada, "HE Sheds A Tear". (Pun Geh
Geh Waazeeben Gwah)
2006 Aboriginal Treasure Exhibit,
Mississauga, ON, Streetsville
Gallery Artist Award for painting
"Sweet Medicine Woman."

Bravery:Aakodeewin

Bravery: facing our challenges with integrity, regardless of the
consequence to oneself, selflessness

1983

*To do what is right even when the
consequences are unpleasant.*

GREAT WARRIOR
The night winds blow
And with them songs
Of tender spirits flow
Ride on great warrior
Of the night
Your battles great
And it is right

REACHING OUT
I look into a face
The image of a place
Of far away
Where children play
And life is just a race
All kinds of games are taught
Like how not to get caught
And how to know
Just when to go
To save you tail from wrought

1983
IN MEMORY OF JOHN PARFREY
RELEASE
*As you reach out to hold me, and your eyes like fire, your
fright is known, you are not who I might still know and I
quiver still the sight I saw....*

To know the horror someone sees
To hold the dead that cuddle me
To hear the songs and chants afar
To hear the whispers of your war
And still I look to see your eyes
So cold and far beyond the skies
Come cuddle close oh warrior dead
The stake be pulled your spirit fed

WOMANS CRY
The spear is high
Yet not as high or loud as a woman's cry
Pierce my soul, vengeful one
Your time has come, my battle won

Bravery:Aakodeewin

Bravery: facing our challenges with integrity, regardless of the
consequence to oneself, selflessness

1987

Bravery:Aakode'ewin-Bravery

*(Many are afflicted with disorders that are secondary to
the initial disability or physical/psychological illness, it is
loved ones that may also be afflicted through long term
issues related to this life of pain and illness.) Feelings in
our environment have a huge influence on oneself and on
others. This can be seen as an intergenerational affect, as in
this child's inability to feel authentically as experienced by
their mother and their mothers' mother, as also the fathers'
teachings re: AUTHENTIC EMOTIONS RELAYED
AT BIRTH AND ONGOING THROUGH THE
DAUGHTER FATHER/MOTHER RELATIONS.*

Daughter

If ever you could see
The rainbow that is made for thee
The glistening night that shines on bright
The silky breeze that makes you squeeze
If only you could see
And yet if you could hear
The tiny ants that build your way
The shining sun that hides the one
The little girl a precious pearl
If only you could hear
And too if you could touch
The highest star would nor be much
The Milky Way would make you sway
And too, the moon would make you swoon
If only you could touch

PRECIOUS TIME

Can you hear it
It's the spirits cry
And the seeking he must do
Can you feel it
It's the cool light breeze
That lures and beckons you
And the turning of a listless face
That stares deep down inside
And the coolness of a sudden hand
That grasps and won't subside
Can you see it
It's the lonely one
That reaches out to you
Can you touch it
It's a chance you take
For to touch is yours to do

Bravery:Aakodeewin

Bravery: facing our challenges with integrity, regardless of the
consequence to oneself, selflessness

(To accept & move toward the spiritual part of death)

FEARLESSNESS

Her tiny hand reaches for the light
And sun appears brushing softly all around her
The tiny tear in her eye
Beckons the wind
And suddenly the air wisps
Her angel face
She smiles and stars appear
Lighting the night with silver dust
Her tiny eyes close
And sleep befalls a little angel
Born of light
Given by day

*(It takes much bravery to face oneself and to allow others
to see also ones pain)*

TIMELESS STARE

The sun shines on her face
of ice
For the tears she's cried
encase her there
She smiles and pieces
fall silent and thrice
Echoing a shattering
timeless stare
A budded rose
she holds so near
Its blooms have fallen
Stem limp and bare
Her tears are flooding
A face of fear
That echoes a shattering
Timeless stare
November 20, 1991

1991
(Numbing is a way of surviving only it distances the
realness within leaving only a shell)

SOLDIER DEAR

Their feet kiss the mud
Their faces kiss the sun
No smile, no laughter
If not for the tiny tear
His face shows nothing
The ticking of his heart
Repeats his every step
Constant, commanding
His voice is only heard within
Screams of agony pierce his flesh
I am human
I am human
Do I not bleed when hurt
Or cry when in pain
When my friend is lying lifeless
A foot away
Do I not reach out to him
And the torn defenseless babies
Do I not cuddle them close
Hear it, the shelling is deafening
Smell it
The charring of the flesh
Face it
Can you feel the sun
Can you hear the laughter
Can you feel
Can you
Their feet kiss the mud
Their faces kiss the sun
No smiles, no laughter
And now no tears

6

Bravery:Aakodeewin

Bravery: facing our challenges with integrity, regardless of the consequence to oneself, selflessness

1991

My Hero
He is my brother
For in his eyes endeared to all
He has a cause
And in that cause is peace on earth
And life to all
For he is my brother
He is my brother
As lifeless body drifting on the wind
And whispers of the numbers called
For he is my brother
A number now is he
He is my brother
As thunder brushes
Mud dried skin
And fires burn
To pierce
A buddy known to all
For he is my brother
Crying freedom for me
He is my brother
For in his arms a baby cries
And songs are sung
And in those eyes
That carry hope and loss
He is my brother
And freedom yet to be

Bravery:Aakodeewin

Bravery: facing our challenges with integrity, regardless of the consequence to oneself, selflessness

(To accept things the way they are and know that one did everything one could at the time)

BABY

The mountains moved today for you the tears they dried to a sky of blue
And a thousand angels wait on high
For you see you've gone and I don't know why
Could it be because you were meant for Him
And the shroud on earth is so cold and dim
For the flowers bend their heads in shame
For her misery and mans cruel maim
Now it's mother earth that blankets you
And the sweet aroma of roses new
For the heavens cry just as I do dear
For your tiny hands and your heartbeat near
February 5, 1992

(As women we may look to others that are powerful role models; this is but one)

JOAN OF ARK

The breath that rides above us lingers silent still
Her heartbeat is the lullaby that drifts atop the hill
Her arms caress our tears away
With silken laden veil
And when she speaks the rumbling's felt
Amongst the harvest sail
Still in this time the pillar reaps
A clone of heavens best
A beauty yet to pierce its dome
And enter mothers nest
Her nurturing instills the sun
And rainbows are her wings
And night turns day
Her breath gives way
For angels songs she sings
Sept 29 1992

Bravery:Aakodeewin

Bravery: facing our challenges with integrity, regardless of the
consequence to oneself, selflessness

1991
We Care

As the reconstruction of a broken vase
A priceless piece endeared to our hearts
You are, my dear loved one
A gem to be shown
As the pieces are slowly but carefully re-assembled
Still you shine
The decor on the surface is only tinsel on the tree
For the vase itself molded by mighty hands
Surpasses any flower with petals drawn
Just as the dew will bend a petal
So does the tears that bow your head
Yet still you are precious
A jewel
Exquisitely shinning
Simple and pure

(Dedication to our soldiers living and dead)
Valor Wed

In the silence of his eyes
Drifts of smoke and battle cries
Armored ox of endless maim
Mounds of lifeless without name
And in the corner of his eye
A touch of angel tears on high
The child is left to fend alone
Amidst the hills of silent stone
For multitudes of flowers red
A soldier true to valor wed.
November 1992

(A fathers love) *his fearlessness when protecting loved ones*
Father

The dawn you kiss with your wingspread wide

As beads adorn your armored chest
And your talons clutch for a fruitful ride
The warrior has come home to rest
Yet in the dark his eyes they see
The dangers lurking closer still
He sets his stake to protect me
With wounded heart and teardrops fill
And in the distance angels sing
The warrior glides his wingspread wide
The beads have turned to silken wing
His talons harbor leather hide
And in his heart are feathers worn
For yet you see he is his own
The warrior lives in silence torn
And thorns upon his head he'll don
November 1992

*(To embrace the next level of life requires leaving that
which may be of comfort. It takes courage to move on into
unknown territory)*
Transition (Womanhood)

The thunderstorm is angels' tears
Her breath she sings a song
A distant brother howls fears
Of disappearing thong
And eagle flies with wounded wing
Her talons stained with blood
She cries a cry of round dance ring
Her speech unopened bud
Atop her head an eagle flies
And lands atop her breast
With feathered armor now she cries
The wind beneath her nest
November 1992

Bravery:Aakodeewin

Bravery: facing our challenges with integrity, regardless of the
consequence to oneself, selflessness

WELCOME INTO MY TEE PEE

A long time ago when my ancestors roamed this
God given earth
We gave thanks to the Great One
We gave back to mother earth, the cedar ashes we
burnt to cleanse the stagnant air and wash the
pollutants out of our place of birch bark walls.
Home we called this abundance of lush greenery
and sparkling turquoise waters.
It has been a long time and we still give thanks,
It is our way to welcome others into our tee pee
And yet we do not ask that you leave your beliefs
at the door
We do not ask or demand that you dissolve your
spiritual rights because you may be welcomed
in our tee pee.
It gives me great joy that for throughout all time we
lived in peace and strength within ourselves. And
our growth is within for Manitou, the Great One,
for He gives us the choice to be honouring Him, or
dishonouring Him. He has given us the power to live
in peace within and with our fellowman. It is our way
of life to welcome all, and not enforce or restrict others
spiritual growth and beliefs.
We honour and respect His word, and His way. Do not
play God; for He gives us choice; and He does
not render His power upon us.
We as a people should strive for such. I welcome you
into my tee pee, so please do not trash that which is my
spiritual strength, but leave if you cannot accept the
boundaries within my tee pee.

1996

*Bravery: Aakode'ewin (it takes much bravery to be able to
laugh at ourselves, humor is our inbred map to survival
and sustenance)*

MOCCASIN WOMAN

Moccasin woman you look so bad
Is it because you lost a shoe in your long travels
Leaving you with callused feet
And pebble ridden toes
How many times have you stubbed that one
Too many times I'd say
And where did you think you were going
Moccasin woman
With that bag of sweetgrass and willow strips
Are they for me
Were you looking for me

1999

*HEALING TAKES MUCH COURAGE, THIS IS A
POEM THAT REFLECTS MY JOURNEY THROUGH
PAIN & SURVIVAL THROUGH LOVE OF
MY CULTURE*

SURVIVAL

Silently I walk alone
The moose hide moccasins my grandmother made me
Guide me to the slow beckoning howl of a lone wolf
He is, as always a guide and true friend
His cries are mine as are his victories
The strength that brushes close beneath his feet
He honors as do I
A vision of solace and acceptance reflects
There; In the moistness of his eyes
For he has lost his way
Just as the moose
There he lunges for the sweetness of release
And yearns for its bondage there in
July 20/99

11

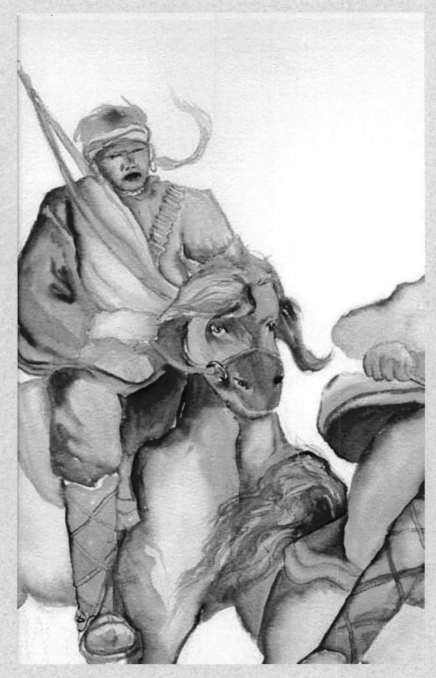

Bravery:Aakodeewin

Bravery: facing our challenges with integrity, regardless of the
consequence to oneself, selflessness

1997

Bravery: Aakode'ewin(persistence and stamina bring a quality that helps us endure. It is a hard realization that one
could go through so much yet benefit good from something so devastating, it takes a fearless heart to
endure all this and more)

TRAIL OF TEARS

In silence I walk
For my leather moccasins are worn
It was a long day but a good one
As we march on; you tell us it is not far to go
We are almost there
And as the sun sets we ready our bow
She comforts the tiny hands that clasp her through the night
And harvest all the tears you say are for our good
You say are for our people
This a trail of tears
A trail of heartache
I look at my young child's face and there is nothing
Generations of inbred stereotype
Bodies with no souls
Souls with no spirit
In silence their protector walks close behind
Tears of long journey`s
Journey`s of destination
Faceless
Destination empty
Destination
Desperation
As sun rises and sun sets so do we
Just as a flower blooms so do we
As rain falls and mist gently rises
So do we
You say it is for our good
We say it is not
In silence we walk
For our leather moccasins are worn
And it was a long day
But a good one.
June 9, 1997

13

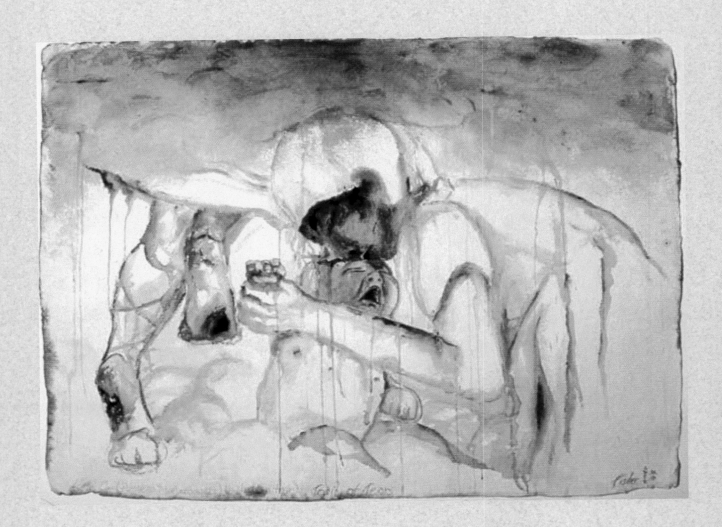

Bravery:Aakodeewin

Bravery: facing our challenges with integrity, regardless of the
consequence to oneself, selflessness

*(Life is but a moment although stopping to hear and see what it really is saying will give one an eternity of memories all
rolled up in one moment of time)*

A Moment in Time

And there I looked across the drive and down onto the grounds
A sense of longing fear I was, at that time overcome
And the heavens cried but in thunderous rage; as if to warn
In times of need
A lion that growls to protect its mate in warning of its property
And as the skies are filled with shattered glass
An instance of a glimpse of He appears to beckon me;
With outstretched arms
He bathes me with everlasting peace and grace
Oh, thunder speaks in angry voice;
Here me sleepy ones, for you are embraced by child of strength
And fierceness, the earth shakes in fear
And the heavens open where light shines bright and beckons silently
And stillness sits in silent bliss
Forever to await the end of one
And the birth of eternity therein
So here I sit peering out upon the grounds
I thank my higher power;
For giving me
A moment in life of heavenly songs
To cherish forever
In a moment in time
May 24, 2000

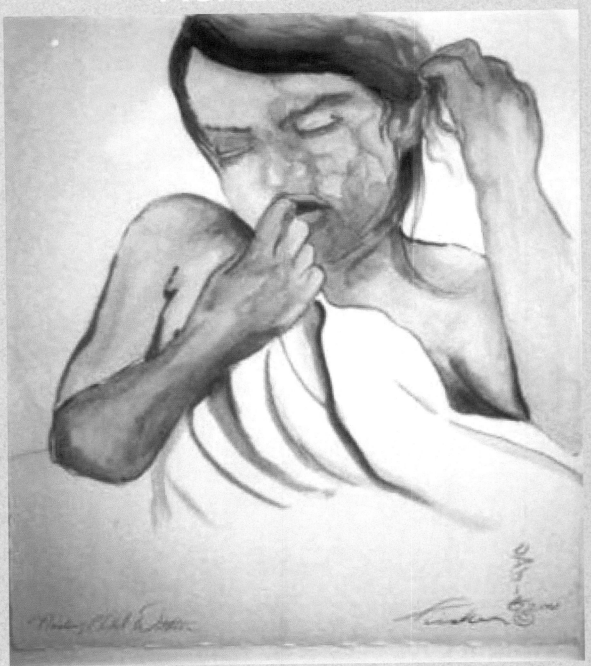

Honesty:Gwayakwaadiziwin

Honesty: facing the world head on, projecting the authentic self
reflects our true eye within eliminating doubt

1992
A NOTE TO MY MOTHER

Mother as you take my hand and guide me
I see your hardships in feathers torn
And the silence that was left inside thee
Your eyes they show the years have worn
But through these years petals fall
The rose it's seeds plants fields of young
And heaven's tears you've cried them all
Your breath it carries wisdom sung
So as I walk with you, hand in hand
Mother, tears of joy cry from my heart
For the roses thrive in the fields of sand
And your silence lends to a work of art
(we watch our children grow and leave our side, we
hope that we have given them the most precious tool in
life, reflecting our honesty and not being afraid to show
them that we too make mistakes and are not perfect,
allowing them also that choice in life.)

RELEASE

She speaks to him of childlike realm
Innocence derived of untouched character
And as the dove nestles close to her breast
A sense of serenity bathes her soul
She is a child and a woman
For her love is truthfully pure
She'll wear the wings of a butterfly
And carry the song of a loon
And in her silence an orchestra plays
Lifting a band of angels
That harbors the child
That rides on the wind.
June 21, 1993

1991
(Acceptance of hardship and grateful for this time in
life)
MOTHERS

Her rosy cheeks blushed
Like soft salmon rose petals
Carefully she brushes away
A wisp of hair
Strands of silk spun with love
The broom she holds now
She clutches with her heart
And music clouds the room
The dance has begun
Silent and gracefully she floats
Endlessly touching every inch
Of the grain filled room
She is lovely in her own way
A beauty unseen b y strangers
The clouds of music lull the heart
They diminish slowly
And the music hushed
She stands alone
Clutching her broom
The day has dawned
The grain filled room still is
And she exits
Content for her heart is of gold
Shinning
Rich and alive

17

Honesty:Gwayakwaadiziwin

Honesty: facing the world head on, projecting the authentic self
reflects our true eye within eliminating doubt

2000

(there may be times when the sludge within can be
overwhelming to the authentic self damaging the
true identity of the person, what I mean are the real
feelings not the masks, numbing the emotions so as to
survive, not having to fear the pain that is excruciating
and disabling . First is to be aware, acknowledge it
and accept the realness within. This only comes with
identifying ourselves through honesty and truth)

STILL I WALK

My shoes are torn and the heal is gone
Still I walk
For to stop would mean
I would have to listen
So I walk and on my many paths
I acknowledge many people
People with wounds and eyes that are
Filled with oceans
Oceans of strife, oceans of pain
And displacement
Oceans of lifelessness
On I walk
And there before me another with a broken
Wing and cannot fly
A prisoner in its own domain
A domain of valleys and hills,
Rivers and paths, so vast
Yet so small, so many,
Yet so few.......
And on I travel,
The many paths are worn
Yet new, as the grass weeps
And brushes my feet, there I walk
Nor to stop
Nor to touch
Nor to feel

May 04, 2000

(Trauma may bring about a close connectedness to the
Creator, spiritual embracement that is like a hick up,
an opening whereby the unconscious objects (issues)
peak out scarring us out of our skins and allowing at
that time an emotional connectedness with our real
authentic selves, OUR INNER CHILD
IS SPEAKING.)

LIKE MOTHER TREE

Like mother tree I stand
Proud and tall ner to fall
Like mother tree I live
To comfort and to give and give
Like mother tree I plan
To impregnate the earth if can
Like mother tree I weep
To give to flowers yet to reap
Like mother tree I smile
When ere you take my hand a while
Like mother tree I wait
For in the end my death be fate
Like mother tree I sound
For there you lay me in the ground
Like mother tree I rise
For there my child around me cries
Like mother tree I am
The sacrificial living lamb
Like mother tree I be
A child within that lives for He
May 29 2000

Honesty:Gwayakwaadiziwin

Honesty: facing the world head on, projecting the authentic self
reflects our true eye within eliminating doubt

*(Honesty comes with listening. Being sure to listen will
allow an honest tongue)*

OLD WOMAN WALKING

Old woman walking
Where are you going
Maa be Sohn you say
Come here
Eh, I will come and listen to what you say
Old woman walking
I will listen
You say your shoes are worn and they are your last pair
You say you are tired and worn like your moccasins
You are silent
And when you speak you speak with a soft voice
Like that of a tiny song bird you sing
And as I look at your worn face, soft eyes
I can only touch on your life of difficulties and strife
shortly
Old woman walking
I hear you
Your hands they tell of many hardships and many loves
Those whom you touched have never forgotten
Those who have felt the hardiness of a hand once
young and strong
Have not forgotten
And as I watch you walking you are frail
and yet;
There is a sense of strength deep inside
Old woman walking
You have taught me well
Even without a word you say something
I listen in awe
For old woman walking
I look down and there on my feet
Are the old worn hide moccasins you so dearly loved
Old woman walking
Wise woman walking

Maa be sohn, I say
Come here little one
Listen to old woman talking
Wise woman walking
Maa be sohn
Maa be sohn

1993

*(protection of our humanism and destructive elements
within, just because we hide them does not mean they are
not seen)*

VANISHING POINT

Her breath glides silent ground unkempt
A mist of breathless tide
And distant drums through hearts that wept
For warriors that have died
Her tears that wash the mud away
From faces that once smiled
We take from her as night to day
We say it's for out child
And when her breath contained in glass
To never kiss the sky
Its bottled seed retained for mass
For warriors yet to die
And faces false that don the pine
We've marred them left for wild
The wind it carries words of mime
We say it's for our child
She cries a rainbow night of day
A halo radiant light
It's warmth it blankets oceans bay
And dove begins its flight
Through forests needn't of her tears
As listless there they lie
And whispers carry on for years
We say it's for our child

20

Humility:Dabaadendiziwin

Humility is not putting oneself higher or better than others, but accepting oneself as equal

1987
CHOICES

We all have choices to a better way of life. As it is short the realization that humbles us is the humility we gain as we realize we are all a part of something much bigger than ourselves.

As time goes on the flowers fade
The sun slowly begins to bade goodbye
And all the while the chance of life eternal
Waits for he who is forever more
With love; life; and choice

THE POWER OF SHE

The darkness evolves endlessly around her as she stands
silently gazing
Her presence is grand amongst the gothic pillars and
marble lion heads
Encircling her body a power envelopes her
And she awaits her destination
Silence is deafening
Just above in the bell tower
An explosion of bells
The lion's roar
And cuddle close to her
She looks down and laughs at the menial surroundings
Her arms outstretched
The power is hers

ONE THE SAME

(knowing oneself as a good part loving and giving the
child also lives within, reconnecting is present)
I see as my heart looks on
You are different
But so am I
And the crumbled leaves
Of many colors fade
We become more as one
The same
The rivers never-ending flow
As your sorrowful eyes they show
And the hurt you feel
As a rabbit caged
I feel too
For we are one
The same
And as night turns to day
And the sun dries the tears
That flow
We will always feel as you
Different
But united as one
For we are one
The same

Humility:Dabaadendiziwin

Humility is not putting oneself higher or better than others, but accepting oneself as equal

(Only when we see ourselves as being equal can we humble ourselves and be human as with flaw.)

HUMBLED

There's times I look into your eyes
And ask myself the question why
I do so much for you; you see
Because I love you so deeply
for times I see myself in you
My question why is answered true
For many tears I've shed in vain
A thousand times I'd do again
December 12, 1991

SPARROWS WHISPER

A sparrows whisper harkens
To an empty valve of mothers' heartbeat
Its` sound a distant muffled cry
Destined to be still
It lives to die
And with each wail
A blanket of silence fills the masses
And fog weighs heavy
On tunes of angels whispers high
Oct. 18/91

(For the old ones)

GRANDMOTHER

Petals fall all around her
Dancing with joy they tickle her nose
Her smile is a rainbow
And gold is her heart

She is old but very young
The hardened lines of age
Soften and she blushes
Like a child
She is not alone
For the many roses she grew
Dance with her
Dropping their petals
They shower her with life
Then bend and give way
For the many new roses to bloom

IN HONOR OF MY CHILD

You look at me
And without words
I know your joy and pain
The many rivers that run dry
Are given by the rain
And when you speak the eagle flies
He watches you my sweet
For rich be gold you shine as this
Amongst the dancing wheat
Nov 20 91

Humility:Dabaadendiziwin

Humility is not putting oneself higher or better than others, but accepting oneself as equal

1993
(At times we may feel that life is heavy and at that time
the end of all things may seem closer than a dream, it
is then we may feel the closest to the Creator and the
Antichrist)

ARMAGEDDON (In My Dreams)
In my dreams
There in a distance a raven glides
And in its beak the eye of heaven dwells
A peace that warms like buffalo hides
I see it in my dreams
In my dreams
A baby cries and wind wisps on
And turtle parched and cracked
Buttercups bend on knee to kiss the crust
I see it in my dreams
In my dreams
The elders still in white buckskin there they lie
They fought the wolves and now sits dove on body torn
And beaded crown adorns their heads
I see it in my dreams
In my dreams
A light so bright it splits the sky in two
And raven falls on scars unearthed by power wars
As mother sighs her last she sings no more
I see it in my dreams

*(This poem reflects the spirit within as one without the
body and immersed completely as unified with the creator
and all His greatness. It is at this time the body does not
exist but only the breath of He)*

HE
And in the midst a mighty wind
It's arms were never-ending
As if to beckon me I walked toward
With open arms I cried
In the name of God I give to Him
My guilt, my shame, my terror within
And as the mighty wind subsides
It takes with it my terror told
And in the silence calmness met
I am embraced with His most high
With Holy Ghost
I shine in peace
And glory to my god I cry
With peace within my spirit rise
And He with me walks hand in hand

Humility:Dabaadendiziwin

Humility is not putting oneself higher or better than others, but accepting oneself as equal

(In harsh times beauty emerges through humbling of others)

TO MY LATE HUSBAND

I sense he is near
There; waiting
His harshness is not his own
And truly there are angels harbored inside
He shall in his silence extend his hand
And in his I lay the bigness of mine
The hurt is mirrored by many
Who wait in radical turn
To penetrate the once baby soft skin
There is flawlessness inside
Quite the opposite of that which is seen
Its reflection only that of a society
Warped and corrupt
It is quite hideous
And yet quite pitiful
The eyes sunken in horrific pain
That would penetrate a nation
So strong is this pain and hurt and despair
That saving oneself would be cruel
Yet in all of this
There lies the sleeping baby
Cuddled and nurtured
Giving birth to a single flower
Of which strength is harbored deep within.
June 16, 2003

Love:Zaagiidiwin

Love: our unconditional love gives peace to oneself and to others

TAKE HEED
Tread soft oh great one
For I am weary
So worn are my lands
So parched are my prairies
My rivers run slow
My quest yet to know
Tread soft oh great one
For I am weary

IT'S OK
Just as the sun peeps through a cloud
And the burst of a newborn flower bud
And the rains above cry a tearful shroud
That blankets all that builds the flood
To see our young begin to walk
And a moment's cry of a mother bore
The first of a muttered word he'll talk
Like the endless grasping of a wave to shore

DARLING
(To my dear husband Real)
I love you
You're the rays of sun
That gently baths my face
I love you
You're the bright lit stars
That led my rightful way
I love you
You're the lullaby
That soothes a troubled heart
I love you
You're the wind and sky

And universal part
I love you
I love you
I've loved you from the start

LITTLE ONE
You speak my child
And with your words
You touch my heart
For you are pure
And none as pure
Could walk the wind
Or shake the earth
Come teach me child
To see and feel
And hear and touch
And thus my spirit sore

SWEETHEART
The time be short so tether not
My love
For time be wrought
My love
I see but not the stars and sky
The moon and sun and earth
But high
Above the things we love
I love you most
My love

FISHER-ODJIG

Love:Zaagiidiwin

Love: our unconditional love gives peace to oneself and to others

DREAMS DO COME TRUE

I slowly slip off
Into a world traveled by many
And the wonders and pleasures
Are now only mine
It is tantalizing
And the hypnotic visions are alluring
For I stop and touch my dream
And wait
You are there

LOVERS

I asked you for a rainbow
The colors were so bright
I asked you for the darkness
You gave me light
I asked you for a soft song
You gave me a lullaby
I ask you do you love me
You gently do reply
I love you you're my rainbow
That beckons me afar
I love you you're my sunshine
That guides me like a star
I love you you're my wind song
That gently wisps my face
I love you dear I really do
Your presence is my place

1987

(There is a constant need for connectedness to the emotions, numbing may create a facade of imitation and a masking of authenticity giving way to never-ending role playing, which can be very exhausting and dangerous)

Love of a mother to her child
We walk far and see much and with it our children also
see through our eyes.
When older and when they are able to view life in the
world as individuals,
it is our influence that carries on in them.
To view from our hearts and connect with our minds is
truth
and strengthens our love to one another for our
children and for ourselves.
Mothers are precious...

COTTON CANDY

The heavens shone like crystal
With clouds of cotton candy she waits
Still no movement or sound
She is a child of unblemished beauty
No faults, no scars
She is new like the crystal
Exquisite
Like the cotton candy she melts into the sky
The clouds are her bed
She is content with that

Love:Zaagiidiwin

Love: our unconditional love gives peace to oneself and to others

(Honoring of my daughter) Children are only loaned to us by the creator, we do not own them

TO MY DAUGHTER

Her face and hands are tiny and pure
The songs that spew from her mouth
Are soft and silent
Her tiny feet like droplets sound
And her eyes that twinkle
Are stars that shine
She thinks only of cotton candy
And the nursery rhymes
Are dancing like rainbows
A graceful dove soars
Then sits upon her shoulder
Content and still
She is life

(being present and aware of our children is essential to our & their well being)

DAUGHTER

You look my way and as you do
A tiny star shoots to the earth
The warm wind you exalt
Warms the ground
Droplets of gold appear
Only then to be swallowed by her
The richness of life springs upward
And orchids fill the breath around
Time stands still
Diamonds reflecting
Are the only movements touched
By the inner eye
A true sense of beauty shared by all
That takes time to stop, look and feel
And see a daughter dear
October 23, 1991

Love:Zaagiidiwin

Love: our unconditional love gives peace to oneself and to others

(Re-connecting to oneself as spiritual enlightenment
brings closer the love of oneself)
HONESTY AND YOUTH
As I look into your eyes
Ocean tides swell
And a fury of distraught winds
Try hurling me to hell
Then soft your hand is sun
A ray of hope and truth
We clutch for only time
Brings honesty and youth
November 6, 1991

(love of oneself and Culture part of self)
THANK YOU
Like the roots of tree to mother earth
I am to thee
As sun to grass
I feel your touch
When ere you pass
And too the rain as mothers tears
Are yet my pain
For night to day as dark to light
You guide my way

"1987
(There is a constant need for connectedness to the emotions,
numbing may create a facade of imitation and a masking
of authenticity giving way to never-ending role playing,
which can be very exhausting and dangerous)
LOVE OF A MOTHER TO HER CHILD
We walk far and see much and with it our
children also see through our eyes.
When older and when they are able to view
life in the world as individuals,
it is our influence that carries on in them.
To view from our hearts and connect
with our minds is truth
and strengthens our love to one another
for our children and for ourselves.
Children are precious..."

YOU GIVE ALL
Your frustration and anger is known by all
And in the break of silence
A breath of air is heard
We are near
For it touches our heart
And warmth billows from all
The many tear drops that fall
Quench the soil we trod
For much is harvested
For mind body and soul
You have given more than you have reaped
For the soil is rich
And the wisdom is deep

Love:Zaagiidiwin

Love: our unconditional love gives peace to oneself and to others

(dedication to my husband Real)

I LOVE YOU

Your ocean eyes they blink
And tiny starlets shoot down your cheek
Your trembling mouth tells me without words
You are hurt and I am sorry
I place my heart around you
And join my ocean tides with yours
And as our cheeks softly touch
The pain is gone
And only peace is ours
November 12, 1991

UNCONDITIONAL LOVE

You look at me
And without words
I know your joy and pain
The many rivers that run dry
Are given by the rain
And when you speak
The eagles fly
He watches you my sweet
For rich be gold
You shine as this
Amongst the dancing wheat
November 20, 1991

(I learned through my husband that letting go was not an option. Flight or fight, I chose to fight. Too many times I chose flight as the feeling of not deserving complete happiness or stability within a healthy relationship was absent. I pushed him away only to pull him back, his pain I could feel, his child I could see and with that I fought for him, I fought for myself. He showed me that abandonment of one's own needs as in love, only feeds the saboteur inside. Through allowing myself to care for my husband I learned that it was possible to care for myself. That I was worthy of love.

MY FRIEND MY HUSBAND REAL

Your face an untold story tells me of your life's pain,
sorrow and strife
The once tiny feet donning papas shoes, are now
travelled well
and flying high on mother butterfly you fly alone.
Just as the hawk your innocence and strength shine
through your eyes
And brother wind carries you far
Whispers tickle your ears telling you stories of
grandfathers songs
These are old but reborn given to the innocence of
mother earth
Time is not silent and the oceans within swell to great
heights
They are strong and helpful and taken as energy
They feed the weakest fawn and strongest buffalo
The boy is now a man
The shoes now fit
And the story now only to begin

Love:Zaagiidiwin

Love: our unconditional love gives peace to oneself and to others

DAUGHTER

There's times I look into your eyes
And ask myself the question why
I do so much for you, you see
Because I love you so deeply
For times I see myself in you
My question why is answered true
For many tears I've shed in vain
A thousand times I`d do again

1992
SISTERS THREE

Below the crystal shinning sphere
A twinkle glistens soft and clear
You walk as mothers' breath you ride
Your hair like eagle feathers glide
And though the waters flow yet still
Your music melts the glacial hill
Its waters flow to bring us light
You are the centre of chrysalis white
Jan 03 92

(unconditional love of mother to daughter and daughter to mother)

A NOTE TO MY MOTHER

Mother as you take my hand and guide me
I see your hardships in feathers torn
And the silence that was left inside thee
Your eyes they show the years have worn
But through these years petals fall
The rose it's seeds plants fields of young
And heaven's tears you've cried them all
Your breath it carries wisdom sung

So as I walk with you, hand in hand
Mother, tears of joy cry from my heart
For the roses thrive in the fields of sand
And your silence lends to a work of art

IN YOUR SILENCE

In your silence the tiny bud falls to the floor
Unopened its beauty still therein
The moon and sun continue on
The seeds of babies born flourish
And the once dormant beauty
Now flourishes with petals drawn
Time goes on and the silent bud unopened
Harvests beauties now shown
Not forgotten is the bud that falls
Unopened and still
Sept 19 1992

SISTER DEAR

The many times I've thought of you
You could not see the tears
For deep inside the hurt was much
Your time was based on fears
My heart went out for one so close
A shadow there I am so near
But cold yet not you warm the heart
Your sunshine's now on rainbows clear
A sister truly
A sister dear

33

Love:Zaagiidiwin

Love: our unconditional love gives peace to oneself and to others

(Love is unconditional good with the bad a fusion of one to the other and in the end every moment is a memory that is frozen in time.)

IN A MOMENT

In a moment I would kiss your cheek
As a snowflake gently does
In a moment I could warm your lips
As the sun its softness was
In a moment I am moved by tears
As rivers surely run
In a moments time I'll love you more
As night and day are one

(My husband Real always called me sweet pea, it is an endearing term, it is special in that our relationship is likened to the perfection of nature)

SWEET PEA

We've danced in the fields of rainbows
Brushed each other at times
Kissed the tears of highs and lows
As wind wisped blossomed rhymes
You flourish fruitful the sweetest of pea
With a butterfly's touch embrace
As a tiny tear drop to sea
Upon your pod its gentle case
We dance amongst the corn husks tall
As sunset touches day
You gently cushion monarchs fall
A blossom felt in May

(The love of oneself to another is without scorn, beautiful and magnificent in its own right)

ROSEBUDS & INNOCENCE

In my silence I remember how your sunshine basked
my soul
Just as the ocean tides, you break against my body
Sending me into a field of roses born
And the rosebud gently blossoms
Brushing its soft petals against my innocence
I tremble, for the innocent are weak with maturity
And a butterfly rests on my breast
With feelings of content
The limpness of my being glides
As wings of eagle flight
And the rosebud blossoms
Burying deep seeds of joy in innocence lay.

(Love of a mate and support when in need of comfort)

HEAVENS TEARS

He sleeps
Just as an unopened bud
His space confined
He cuddles his dreams
Without hesitation or regret
A star touches his shoulder
Kissing it dearly
And the gold dust left
Adds to his sensation
He wakes to angels' songs
And heavens tears create a blossom
Endeared by star and all
Who are without regret

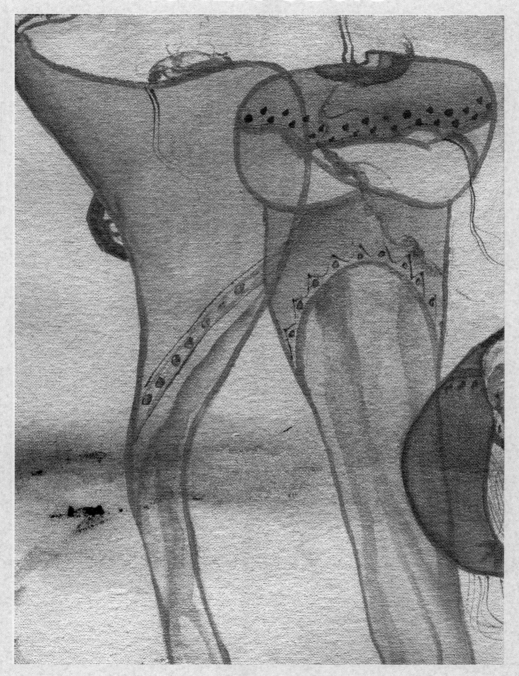

Love:Zaagiidiwin

Love: our unconditional love gives peace to oneself and to others

(There were many storms this year and many stands to take toward fight or flight feelings)

UNCONDITIONAL LOVE

The butterfly waits
Nestled faithfully in a mountain of stone
She is content
For the storm it's ravage bore
A mighty stand he waits
For slowly his heart appears
Like baby doe
The shyness is
And the butterfly soothes
Dancing to the calm instilled
As both elude the storm
And become one
A chrysalis born
June 17, 1993

THANK YOU MON AMOUR

I sit and watch you
You are serene
No cruelness about
Your hands are star dust and Milky Way
And as they move with the wind
My body is lifted amongst heaven's gate
I await your presence
For your great wing comforts me
And your tender heart speaks to mine
We travel heights known to rainbows
And with this as our path
Together we share the gold
As one we are

(The need to be loved without question, as trauma isolates a person's ability to trust, it is only the self and inner child that really understands its affects. Being isolated from ones Culture can be very lonely, looking at the brighter side is looking at the added drive the anger may instill.)

OH GRANDFATHER

I hear a distant drum
It beckons me to come
And songs of long ago
The wind it carries low
I dance upon the sun
Remembering my run
Through apple orchards fine
Remembering that time
Oh grandfather old
Your song is told
And eagle sits to right
Your shoulders set to fight
The tears are shed by small
And babies' cry for all
The talons carry way
Remembering this day

(Love spins many webs but few know its value and construction)

PERSISTANCE

A broken window awaits
The widowed spiders' song
And a symphony begins the day
Of a love that's oceans long
Of a love that's tried and strong

Love:Zaagiidiwin

Love: our unconditional love gives peace to oneself and to others

(In times of loss there enters the feeling of abandonment, not only of someone dear but this can also apply to the abandoning of oneself.)

LOST ONE

In a silence born of rose
Visions enter light
Tiny teardrops dance on toes
Heaven is your plight
And in the night the gales do sing
A thrashing they befall
Hand in hand a flower ring
A gesture known to all
Your sun shines through the eye of storm
Your hands they cradle two
And eagle flies his wings be born
His talons stained of dew
For rainbows touch a heart of might
And teardrops dance of sun
And night shall be the light of day
To harbor all as one
Just as the mother cradles son
Brother owl shrieks
Its cape endowed with feathers none
Lest harbor raven speaks
As son rides high upon its back
Mother wind prevails
A silent whisper touches fact
A field of cattails whale

SISTERS

The gentle touch of your hand
Nurtures my soul as the great eagle
And as he
You wrap your mighty wings
To harbor those you love
A rainbow circles your path
Giving way to diamonds uncut
And brother tree shelters you
From earthly wolves that seek
Yet quietly you float on clouds
Of silken lace
For you are the wind carried high
The angels dance your song
And like sister sun
Your warmth is deep from within

LOVE

In times of toil the owl sits
On shoulders laden still
The mountains move for you my dear
The wind is high and nil
A whisper soothes your burdened heart
And time wraps bows of love
The eagle is your shadowed cape
For love surrounds like dove
I touch your heart as mine you do
And precious petals lay
You are my early morning sun
My virtuosic by day
July 27, 1993

Love:Zaagiidiwin

Love: our unconditional love gives peace to oneself and to others

1998
Birthday

A birthday is the birth of a newborn
The sparkling wide eyes of an innocent child
The growth of a tiny person who in time becomes big
The many hours of developing into a monarch
butterfly
A birthday is the birth of a human
The light of the sun, wind, and flourishing of a new
bud
The essence of timelessness, and yet
The growing of young to old
And in that time of struggle and ease
There is the developing of a human life
Through time the many happy birthdays sing
And the songs are many
For if it were not for these songs
The multitudes of endurance, sustenance, and grace
Would not be known
We live to experience these teachings of life
And grow to believe that through it all
Our birthday will be a happy birthday
For the love of others and of ourselves
Can only be, with the life we are inside
For the happiness we cherish along the long road of
Many happy birthdays
And many struggles therein

1999

*(Memories are a huge and important part of who we are
and allow us refuge from the harshness of life, they are
stepping stones of wisdom gifted to our generations, they are
also healing visuals a symbol of our paths walked, yet even
though we may not remember them they still exist within
our unconscious at times peaking out and delightfully
surprising us)*

MY MEMORIES

My memories are a part of you and me
They are the little cries and boisterous laughter
When looking at your accomplishments and not
They are looking up and seeing the brightest star
When looking at your wide eyes shining
And the laughter as it poured from your tiny lips
Memories are forever
They are a history of your many paths
A first step and arms that hug and grasp the nose
Upon my face
They are eyes that welcome your first step
From baby shoes to runners laced with sparkles too
They are Tommy shirts and crinolines
And bunny rabbits
Snuggled in amongst the others you so loved
The memories are many
As that vivid part of them I see
The kitty cats you loved so dear
The scrapes and cuts upon the knees
Two delicate hands that grasp the roses now
You hold in front of you
Memories, they are but a precious part of me I keep
And as you grow and slowly journey on your path
ahead
You too will welcome your very own part of memories
to keep
For memories are cherished as such
A timelessness we create
That harbors within us the many experiences
Endured and not forgotten

Love:Zaagiidiwin

Love: our unconditional love gives peace to oneself and to others

2000

(The loss of emotions are a dangerous thing as it is the emotions and feelings that allow us a healthy response to decisions a healthy drive and motivational plain, if we were to be robots made of tin and hallow inside we could and would do anything without the fear of consequence. This is what trauma does stuffs and shields our emotions to the extent of inaccessibility, this is dangerous.)

EUPHORIA

I awake, yearning for the touch of dew to ever so lightly
Place itself like a velvet glove upon my skin
I ready myself quickly
So as to be within my element
Without human consumption
My walk is sure and in haste......
For I yearn to wake the natures calm and
Rise in pureness like mother sun
With arms outstretched and grasping
The scents of blossoms pierce my nostrils
And the fragrance massages my every pore
The grass clippings of fresh mulch bath my every step
And as my boot descends on a blossom picked,
It lifts me up and into another world of honor and grace
The valves of desire permeate every inch of my being
Rising me to ecstasy a princess born of light
And as I walk the grounds of Mother earth
The raven lifts me to a castle of regal state
And it is there I sit at heaven's gate
To hear, smell, touch and feel the complete
Amalgamation of serenity within.
May 6, 2000

2001
BROTHER AND SISTER

I want to tell you something
I want to tell you that the sun shines bright
And warms all the night
I want to tell you
About the day I awoke and thought of you
And how lucky I am
To have brothers and sisters
And when I sleep
I relish all the memories stored delicately
In a beautiful box with a bow
The memories of your big smiling eyes
And loving hugs
Of the wonderful walks we had
And all the laughs, cries and concerns we experienced together
I want to tell you
That in the times of sadness
Your funny, loving jokes lifted me and the darkness there lit up
Like rays of sunshine filtering through a tunnel
Long and dark
And the rainbows filled your footprints
Lifting us high
And you reached to grab my hand
And together we ran in fields of stars

Love:Zaagiidiwin

Love: our unconditional love gives peace to oneself and to others

(A dedication to my cousin and all men who have
experienced trauma)

BROKEN CHILD WITHIN

How broken are you old man
That I cradle you as a babe in arms
How broken are your eyes and heart
That I hold you so dear
Like mother tree nestled safe on limb
How broken you are
I nurture and soothe you
And you drink the milk that shields your soul
How broken you are
Old man
Young man
How broken
Tell me old man
What were you feeling
When all alone, no voice you had
No soul you weep
And as you embrace that warrior within
Do you hold tight the armour
You've so learned to wear
You've so learned to love
Your castle with its high and mighty walls
Are almost impenetrable
But that's what you need old man
A haven of safety and solace
Where you are the controller
And you are the victim
Yet deep in that castle far below
The depths of its stones
There sits a little boy naked and torn
Frightened of all or any that enter the room
There where he sits all curled and confused
Yes, old man
You are a child within
And an adult without

And deep down time comes
When the little boy breaks through
the wall of stone
Side by side
Hand in hand
With the old man broken
And the young man transformed to carry on
And carry out his lifelong dream
Of being who he is and always was
That little boy playing in the sunlit dawn
Happy old man of wisdom and joy

"GOD MADE ME, NOT THE WAY YOU SEE ME
BUT THE WAY HE MADE ME".
*Love: Zaagiidiwin-To know Love is to know peace. Love
must be unconditional. (When people are weak they need love
the most. Love of oneself is to be whole and content with the
Creator as unconditional love takes precedence over
earthly reign.)*
And the sky's opened and a bright light pierced my eyes,
the rays grasping me around my body. I feel warmth so
penetrable it makes my soul sing. Angels voices hearken
to its' soothing song, a song of many tongues, a song so
majestic and clean, the words non-determinable, it races
through, rebuilding every molecule around, transforming
them into one unified being. The greatness is spellbinding
and as I look, my hands outstretched I give my heart
and soul, there in front in all its'glory the many faces of
she, engulfed in halo's of gold our tears brush and fall
to the sand, crystallized in perfect oneness; round, like a
diamond cut of perfection, they moisten the earth and
bring forth the perfect life everlasting never to be touched
by human hands nor to be reformed or defaced; but to
forever dance on silken sand transformed forever.

Love:Zaagiidiwin

Love: our unconditional love gives peace to oneself and to others

2008
CHANGES OF LIFE

There in the beauty of all that is sacred
A fineness of intricacy only to be held in all its glory
Refined in gold and relinquished in stories of all
The richness of old and new tattered in finery of
distant faith
A warmth of rivers known only to few
Within, there sits awaiting the birth of new
Against the crushed leafs of yarrow and cedar
The fragrance is strong but soothing to within
It basks against the bark and runs free as oceans are
to flow
A light of endless purity and ever not to be still
Crashing still to boundless fear a haven of ecstasy born
by light
Down to crevasses, mounds of ancient bliss
Filled within the porous mounds it travels fervent
without cause
Around the forks of streams and roots of barbarous
terrain
Following a path that is made by unnatural means
Ribs of parched anger it billows over with haste
Toward the eminent lions it stalks
Rains beat down on hallowed out frowns made by
hearts of steal
And in all its fervor
Plant yet another seed within

1983
LIFE

I look into the deepest pool
And still my hand I reach
For nothing be too far or near
That I may touch or teach
The hole is deep and dark inside

And hesitate I may
Yet life is full of chance and change
That I may live this day

IN MEMORY JOHN C. PARFREY

When the look of life is washed away
Hands and face there listless lay
Clothing neat and placed just right
Is it really you I see in sight
Though the smile you wear is yours my dear
I hesitate to come too near
Hands that gently fold on your chest
The look is one of gentle quest

(Having respect for one another gives power to
whatever is needed to move through the many
challenges couples may entail)

AS ONE

You stand as one sharing the same stem
Your lips touch close as the petals of a rose
Yet to bloom
Your arms entangled in each other as vines
Reaching for eternity
Your thoughts are as one thought
Strong and alive
Just as the root of the rose
A lovely vine
All part of the tree of life
You stand together

Respect:Minaadendamowin

Respect of life is essential as accepting ourselves as gifts from our Creator a humbling reality.
In order to earn respect you must give it, embracing all life as important and imperative internally and externally for a well balanced self

1991
SYMPATHY

At times we gaze into a void
Nothing enters
And nothing leaves
Time stands still
For there is no heartbeat
Just the constant vibration
Of mother earth
Even the tiniest grasshopper
Is silent and still
And when a petal falls
Its' sound is echoed
For even the fragile bruising
Of a flower
Is heard
And time stands still once more
In honor of its beauty and strength
November 1, 1991

EVOLUTION

As buffalo`s float like smoke from fire
The orchids bloom with teardrops stained
My friend the eagle soars much higher
The sun grows old where teardrops rained
The blades of grass are bent and crying
Fields of cattails whip her face
Mother's dress now browned and dying
Frozen tears fall trimmed in lace
One of four now reigns in torment
Bear cub slumbers close to spring
Fire nears and water is sent
Floods of tears roll down her wings

(We must give respect to earn respect, this can be done through respecting elders for their gift of wisdom and truth, for we do not know everything)

FOR THE OLD ONES

As I am embraced by mother earth
Her grandeur cuddles me
and keeps me warm
Her breath carries songs
and they are comforting to my ear
The drum I hear is of old songs
My grandfather sang
But only now do I here
Echoes of past spirits
Their heartbeat fading
But not completely
For the eagle carries the old songs on
And the drum she is singing
Grandfathers' song

1992
SISTERS

Below the crystals shining clear
A twinkle glistens soft and dear
Your walk as mother's breath you ride
Your hair like eagle feathers glide
And though the waters flow yet still
Your music melts the glacial hill
Its waters flow to bring us light
You are the centre a chrysalis white

Respect:Minaadendamowin

Respect of life is essential as accepting ourselves as gifts from our Creator a humbling reality.
In order to earn respect you must give it, embracing all life as important and imperative internally and
externally for a well balanced self

1993
*(Respect creation as it gives life, like that of a woman,
mother & wife)*

WHEN EAGLES FLY
When the eagle flies
I'll take your hand
And guide you to a place
Where velvet stones caress your hair
And oceans trimmed in lace
When time eludes the wings of wind
And carries cattail seeds
To ever whisper thunder storms
That ravage nature's weeds

*(respect for a sister going through much pain a pain that
is invisible to the eye, we see a man without a leg we feel
for him, but, someone grieving deeply we just pass by, and
shake our head.) I have great respect for those who harbor
invisible wounds*

FORGIVE ME
I cried today for you
Like sister loon
And in the silence of my heart
A broken feather dons my hair
For distance cradles song unsung
And brother eagle dances to
The breath unleashed by mother wind

*(the respect of a father who carries much pain reflective of
the many soldiers who died and also lived in a world much
their own after the war.) I give great respect to my father.*

DADDY SWEETGRASS
In your eyes I see brother eagle
He watches you my sweet
In your voice I hear the loon
He rides beneath your feet
And in the distance a drum it sings
For endless songs unsung
Your carried high by winds great wings
Awaiting feathers hung
Your chest adorned with silent beads
With leather crown secure
And moccasins that brush the seeds
Of harvests meant to cure
The beetles dance amongst your feet
A rainbow hugs the sun
And sweet grass wisps amongst the wheat
To cushion feathers hung

Respect:Minaadendamowin

Respect of life is essential as accepting ourselves as gifts from our Creator a humbling reality.
In order to earn respect you must give it, embracing all life as important and imperative internally and
externally for a well balanced self

(giving respect gets respect, there may be a time when the thought of receiving something worth while is not considered viable for those who dance in devils shoes, it's easy to ignore and stuff and hide the bad one, but that only makes for more anger)

RECOVERY.

In the silence of my heart I hear
The legends spoke
The inner eye rapes ocean tear
Elders' visions stoke
Behind my head an eagle flies
He carries mothers' seed
And sister loon gives way to cries
In harvest time of need
Now silent star dust basks my face
A richness I befall
And heavens wings are angel lace
A time given to call
So listen well as old ones speak
Their talons yet be drawn
For rich be poor and strength be weak
The fox is silent brawn
June 27th 1993

(All creation should be treated with respect and honor, this we give to our children and child within; as others have pain we may also feel that pain. Empathy is a blessing and without it we would not feel beyond our own selves.)

DARLING

I wanted you to know that in these times of trouble
My heart reaches out beyond the boundaries sometimes
set
By experiences untold
For the real pain felt is also felt by me
The timeless hours spent in constant worry
I feel too
For you are made of the same
As your father and his father
The feather of the eagle is sacred
And the breeze is much cooler
On the wings of an eagle
With feathers intact
Honor him with not one feather
But with the cool breeze of wind
Beneath your wings
July 01, 1993

Respect:Minaadendamowin

Respect of life is essential as accepting ourselves as gifts from our Creator a humbling reality.
In order to earn respect you must give it, embracing all life as important and imperative internally and externally for a well balanced self

(Honor of those who have left us early; we honor their travel now into Mother Earth who will embrace them on their journey into the next life)

HEAVENS CHILD

The heavens cried their tears today
And oceans made their beds
For out of sky the diamonds dance
The cattails nod their heads
And silence whispers secrets near
While monarch spreads its wings
To fly amongst the baby dear
Then flutter close to kings
And mountain top cries thunder storms
That move beneath the feet
Of tiny beetles harvest dorms
On sun kissed harvest wheat
July 28, 1993

BATTLE CRY

Your silence is a battle cry
You whisper into night
Your cloak don with shining star
And feathers are your plight
The eyes that look are eagle born
As feet are talons told
You glide by night and sleep by day
Your stories left for old
And when you speak the flowers bloom
In sunlit heavens dorm
For raindrops fall to quench a thirst
And dance to manmade storm

Respect:Minaadendamowin (in times of grief and loss support and comfort is needed as the person is raw and without skin, vulnerable and therefore defensive) There is a cry for those who may feel deceived who give but do not find the empathy in return.

WARRIOR CRY

When dust it settles there you sit
Amongst the broken hearts
Above the rays of golden blitz
Adorn the rubble parts
The wind it carries warrior chants
Of chieftains long ago
And broken promises enhance
The life of picture show
You talk to me in buffalo hide
That's made of silken thread
Above a metal bird you ride
Adorned by vulture head
You carry not a talking stick
But brandish hardened steel
You carry deep a heart of gold
And ride on medicine wheel

Respect:Minaadendamowin

Respect of life is essential as accepting ourselves as gifts from our Creator a humbling reality.
In order to earn respect you must give it, embracing all life as important and imperative internally and
externally for a well balanced self

2002
THERE SITS SHE
There sits she
Waiting like a monarch she huddles constricted
In a world so huge, oh, so much bigger than she,
yet; there waits she
For not far off sits he
Arms embracing chest, moisture making way down
his cheeks, too long waits he
waits he too long
And at this time
Mother wind pipes up
My children it is time
And kissing both; the crystals fall
For it is time,
Time it is, she cries
For all to see, the beauties made for beauty shared,
Is but that which God hath made
So share like that of beauty seen
For sharing is a beauty given
Remorse; the shell of hardened case
For beauty lies in silent wait
Be gone the shell of ugly flesh
Emergence of a tiny tear to roll on down
Upon the flesh
It's blossom scent erodes the shell
To make emerge a beauty so grand,
So grand are they
Our breath is stilled,
we sigh
We share a moment from within…
01/2/02

Respect:Minaadendamowin

Respect of life is essential as accepting ourselves as gifts from our Creator a humbling reality.
In order to earn respect you must give it, embracing all life as important and imperative internally and
externally for a well balanced self

2003

*(Our children are only loaned to us, a sacred part of our
Creator; we respect them as we too shall then be respected)*

INSTILATION OF HOPE

Hope is the sun coming over the tree top
The laughing of children
The smile of an old one
Hope is the dancing of a little boy
And a little hand in a big one
It is an old woman and old man
Still saying Ì love you`
And sitting and watching the ocean
Kiss the shore
Hope is looking to the future
For happiness that comes
From the freedom to choose
It is reaching out
And realizing that there's someone there
Hope is for everyone
From small to big
And back again to small
Hope is for a future
With the human race
That knows not everything
But knows oneself
October 19/03

2008

(Spirits in the Longhouse) Visions within the spirits
roamed within the walls of Crawford Lake

CRAWFORD LAKE

As I walk my moccasins kissing mother earth
I walk in haste to reach my destination soon
It is yet dark and all around the ravens glide
The crows yak at my presence strong
I reach the entrance on the west side
There welcomes me her face
She sits atop the fallen tree
Ahneen-Se:kon-Hello
For welcoming my humble spirit
I continue to a place that is of great strength
The sun yet asleep
I take from my bag my stone
Sweetgrass, cedar and sage
I am at one with all as the spirits
Dance laugh and sing
They are not fearful of the newcomer
The woman craving to know
I squat to start the sacred smoke
It melts upon my body
And enters through my nostrils
The sweetness flows within
Like a rushing stream
Enticing to my old soul
I close my eyes and they dance
And welcome me home

Truth:Debwewin

Truth:Debwewin ahh to be oneself honest and true

1993
(Do not deceive others intentionally as they may question every step you take)

FALLEN ANGELS

The sky lit as a rainbow glides
Her arms outstretched she sings
Her breath the wind cries ocean tides
She's lost on eagle wings
The oceans part for her they say
You are like we the earth
Your feet shall rest on silent day
Your heart it joins our birth
The heavens burst and angels sing
Her spirit glides as they
Her foot of talon breaks the ring
To circle new this day
They say you are not what you are
Yet turn away their face
Their hands be paws confined in bar
Their hide has turned to lace.

Feb 1993

(We speak truths as the wind relays what we want to hear we must listen intently if we are to hear the truth) Masks are many but blur the truth to ourselves also.

BROTHER

You are my brother fox
And like the wind your scent deceives
Just as I our predators seek
Mother wind carries us far
The rivers flow to cover our tracks
Hide as we ourselves from they
And in the night of day
You speak to me
Then pause
And walk with midnight sun

(Forgiveness of our limitations and acceptance that there are times we need to trust others for help because there are some things we cannot do alone)

I SURRENDER ALL

So here I sit amongst all God's children
Amongst leafy limbs that reach out to hold, yet here I sit
Safe amongst myself
I harbor all my pain
All my grief
All my sadness.
I have yet to surface the anger rage and bitterness I shield from
What I do not know
And why I do not know
For what I have built around me to protect the child within
Withstands any attack that I know I have built on my own
And as the attacks come forth
And tiny pieces crumble to the ground
I hurry to replace them with more impenetrable substances
And as I know this wall of anger, rage pride and pity
Withstands all and any attack
I stand alone, for humility must be my friend
And pride my enemy
He only shall permeate my wall
And when I reach out to take that hand
Then and only then shall the wall crumble
And there I stand with shield and armor around my feet
And trust there clenched in hand
I surrender all I can
I surrender all I will
I surrender all

May 6, 2000

FISHER-ODJIG

Wisdom:Nibwaakaawin

Wisdom: embracing knowledge as gifted by the Creator and using it for
the betterment of the self and others

*(The Creator gives us tools of which with wisdom we share
through our spiritual enlightenment and teachings that we
are small but powerful)*

SON

With great hands outstretched he held the sun
And warmth radiated in exalted beauty
The raven glides close only to perch on his shoulder
The clouds parted and rays of gold showered upon him
And when he clapped his hands the heavens cried
And thunder broke unleashing a vengeance that echoed
The waves then parted a path and son was born
Radiant too, like silver bolts
He now is and always was
Oct 26/91

(We can learn from our friends of the forest)

CELEBRATION

Dance
Dance my young one
Like the partridge
You pound the earth to wake her from her sleep
Your demands reflect your hunger
And as you soar high above the mother of life
Your wings carry you to spread tradition and unity
For your people await to feel the breath of life from
your great wings
And the strong beat of your heart lifts many to soar
as you
The great eagle you are
Miigwetch

LITTLE ROCK

Oh, little one
You see me

So beautiful
So round
So smooth
So sparkly
I have lived long and seen much
I have heard much
Many have cuddled me in their hands
They honored me
By skipping me across mother waves
There I have lain looking up
Through the silken waters
And through time these treacherous waters
Have tossed me back and forth
To and fro
And I am left at times
Still
In the mud
Yet I am thankful
For without all this
I would be easily chipped and broken
Without the troubled waters
I would not have these smoothed corners
I would move with difficulty
Ah……. But alas
Now I move with grace, ease and power
For I am well rounded
You toss me over the rippled waves of mother water
Only for her to gently caress me back to shore
I thank you and mother waves
For giving to me
That which I may not have had
A well rounded circle of life
Ongoing, never-ending, challenging and good
Miigwetch

Wisdom:Nibwaakaawin

Wisdom: embracing knowledge as gifted by the Creator and using it for
the betterment of the self and others

*(Dedication to my deceased husband in honor of his
selflessness for a cause,it is wise to look at others pain)*

WARRIORS HONOR

With blankets rolled against his chest
His voice within is silent still
And eagles fly just as he rests
A soldier fighting for a will
Yet hands of listlessness reach out
We turn away as not to see
And eagle soars without a doubt
His cries are heard from sea to sea
For yesterday he ran and played
Like brother bear and sister deer
And angels wings bend hither bade
To rest beside his Godly mirror
It's time the songs they whisper hymns
Of reconciliation meant
His silence is of quiet limbs
The will has left the soldier sent
November 1992

*(The many things given by the Creator are seen also in our
environment and its occupants animals, plants,
rivers and air)*

GREAT WHITE PINE TREE

The great white pine tree whispers my name
For her tears are there on a face so bare
And her once fine cloak is so torn and old
Oh great white pine tree whispers so low
And great white pine tree her arms outstretched
She says that her brothers have been taken away
And she's lonesome and frightened for her babies
some day
For where will great eagle mother harbor her young

Oh great white pine tree whispers on
The great white pine tree whispers your name
Come sit and rest in my shattered breast
And remember when I gave you this place
Oh great white pine tree with tears from her face

BEGINNING OF THE END

The air around like golden bands
Mould to my body
The clouds like cotton candy cushion my flight
Time speeds on then moments before descending
It pauses and great hands engulf me
Placing me safely on the ground
Mother earth wraps her arms around me
There is no need for heat
For I am warm
There is no need for food
I am not hungry
There is no need for air
For I am breathless
Mother earth is now my comfort
I feel no pain

Wisdom:Nibwaakaawin

Wisdom: embracing knowledge as gifted by the Creator and using it for
the betterment of the self and others

1993

*(The Creator and spirituality cries for recognition and there
sits a tug of war between religion and culture, (Christianity
and Cultural Identity) The struggle continued until peace
within as Christianity was my religion and my Cultural
Identity established a sense of earthly connectedness. The
fusing of 2 objects simultaneously existing together in unison
allowed peace.*

MOTHER SWEETGRASS

The Sweetgrass moans beneath the feet
Of moccasins white as snow
And gently there the roses bend in tears
The feathers don a braided crown
As ribbons would a bow
And eyes of eagle talon harbored fears
The essence of a song that rides abreast the breath of wind
Of silent psalm is carried in its right
And tongues that carried legend tales are cast of those who
sinned
Are singing now the warriors song of might.

1994

*(As identity is important to relay it to our young is vital to
their acceptance of who they are and where they will go, we
must seek wisdom to gift it to our children)*

CULTURE WAITS

In your heart young one we see life
But time has tainted your cloak
And eagle glides where culture waits
And you dance each step there petals fall
Till in time the flower is no more
And all that is left is cracked and dry
For this we see the devils reign
For as elders we try to change it
And as children you will.

1999

TIMES TO COME

It came upon time that man would devour man, and all
of Gods creatures would be still. A time when day turns to
night, the deafening sound of emptiness, a void so great,
it pierces everything around. Movement becomes nil and
the tiniest of insects are not heard. A stillness so grand,
yet frightening, until the heavens begin their journey
of song, a song of conviction and wrath, a song of long
awaited and prophesy so horrendous and so foretold,
that the greatest of man shivers. Blankets of hail, the
size not experienced ever, of waters parting, and spilling
over every living thing, winds greater than the greatest,
never to be seen, never to be believed, viciously sting
everything in sight like that of a thousand locusts. The
sinners, the non-believers, wallowing in torched oceans of
tides suffocating with scorched fires, fires of endless pain,
afflictions so devastating and so devouring that in only
minutes the screams are hushed, are no more, are gone.

It is at this time heavens will open, the dead shall rise,
their restoration of human form, of Christian delicacy, is
restructured into a vision of everlasting beauty, and grace.
Their eyes starlit and mirror's of a face so beautiful, so
gracious, so sinless, to turn away would be sinful. Their
bodies incomprehensible to human existence, a being
so foretold yet so forgotten, floats high into the opening
of a gloriously opened sky. A sky, only to be viewed by
the forgiven, the meek, the without sin. And when the
heavens part, music, like a thousand orchestras' sound,
exploding with reverberation, so piercing to the heart,
it will make you faint and float like sweetgrass soothing
the face and cuddling the heart. It will give a new life, a
new form of molecular significance, a new form of Godly
existence that permeates every Godly thing. A moment
in time, like the blink of an eye, the birth of followers
of Christ, the birth of the reborn, and the death of the
antichrist. The ever existing Holy power of GOD and
His Omnipotence.

Wisdom:Nibwaakaawin

Wisdom: embracing knowledge as gifted by the Creator and using it for
the betterment of the self and others

1987

(Let go of the expectations and enjoy the gift of others)

FORGIVENESS IS A SMILE AWAY

You turn your head toward me as if to say you're sorry
But it's nothing you have done
Nothing you have said
Can the stars vanish yet so bright
Not with the night but with the day
Yet then again the cycle is a blank
A yawn, a heartbeat high
The time is not but timeless space
A tear it dries without a trace
So fear not
What you see is not
The tears are gone
The smiles are sought

1993

*(cherish knowledge and wisdom and know where it
comes from)*

OLD ONE

Old one I look at you
And in your eyes an eagle cries
And the grass its dew
Reflects as the tiny stars that harbor skies
Old one I feel for you
For legs that sit like old pine tree
And rivers cry too
As they sink beneath the canyons sea
Old one I love you
Just as the sun in need of moon
And laughter new
From echoed cries of misty morning baby loon

*(Listen and take note that our wisdom comes from our
elders lips, wisdom comes from them what they have is
given to us and our children)*

OLD WOMAN I SEE IN YOU

Old woman I see in you
The eagles' eye
And in its flight
The scent of mother earth
The sweet grass cries
Old woman I feel in you
A frightened hare
The stormy paths
And hawthorn arms
Embrace as if to care
Old woman I hear you cry
Like sister loon
And in its song
A lullaby whispers high
Enchanting tune
Old woman I am you
Like bud in bloom
A flower once
In wisdom heir to stone
Its petals strewn

Wisdom:Nibwaakaawin

Wisdom: embracing knowledge as gifted by the Creator and using it for
the betterment of the self and others

2000

CEREMONY (CLEANSING)
THE HEALING

As I enter the room its fragrance soothes my soul
I am safe, warm, and protected
The smiling eyes of one so blessed and gifted
I am content to sit
You give me a feather in hand and my eyes meet yours
You gently place your hand on shoulders torn
And in that moment of song
I weaken with deliverance cloaked
And float on high where buffalo roams
The feather clenched released my pain
And with that moment I collapse into the medicine wheel you stand
There with song you bask from me
And draw the hate and hurt and pride
You take from me replenish I
For eagle perched upon your back
You feed me new and harvest clean
I am drawn down from buffalo skin
And lay with feather upon my chest
Released, with turtle beneath my feet

Wisdom:Nibwaakaawin

Wisdom: embracing knowledge as gifted by the Creator and using it for
the betterment of the self and others

*(In our soul dwells our emotions as they are meant to be
one, it is wise to listen to what our spirit has to say)*
ONE WITHOUT THE OTHER
The soul is no doubt the basis of our lives
And the heart is no doubt the sleeve in which it sits
One without the other cannot exist
But rather wither and crumble to the ground.

DAPHNE (to my aunt)
Oh, sweet old woman wise old woman
I see in your almond eyes
The oceans sing
And on your head a crown there sits
Oh, sweet old woman wise old woman
And there in hand a dove awaits
Your name it sighs on winds above
So whisper low, oh sweet old woman
My ears are perked for knowledge wise
Your hand an eagle feather waits
To paint your journey`s path in stone
You carve the canvas trail of tears
Of sculptured lines and pools that mirror
Emeralds, diamonds, gold and myrrh
As eagle feather paints the path
Of sweet old woman, wise old woman
Born of raven, eagles eye
Harboured in the silken skin
Of fisher running wild

2007
(We can learn much by listening)
IN THE BEGINNING
In the beginning there was plant, animal and mother
earth
A vision of beauty through eyes that held her in highest
regard
There was peace, harmony and respect in her wisdom
and grace
He also of the highest regard and essence of spirit
Fathered the greatest of son
And with it came a unified structure
Impenetrable in thought
Many moons passed as all basked in celebrations
So vast that in its infinite glory
There was no end
As the growth of many great roots flourished
There came with it floods, droughts, famine and fear
Fear that the harvests once had
Would be lost
There was the hardened silence of wind
And the eagles were few
The great white bear harbored gills so as to survive
And the once glorified sense of being frayed
As the red, white and blue blankets
Weakened and encased safety no more
Many moons dissolved into day
Washed by a veil now void of any realness
A realness of life taken by our own hands

Words as symbols through ceremony, ritual, humor, and art have aided the First Nations people on many forms of emotional and feeling plains, a universal derivative of cultural awareness to healing within.

Native art encompasses a picture that is circular, which has no limitations of time or space. It is a continuous plain, a storyboard, a scroll of visual activity and primary process thinking, that in which nature projects as a survival instinct.

Native people view life in a more holistic and natural sense. The circle was and is a way of life, which to the First Nations is unending, and ever existing, and perfect. Within it exists a line of balance, a middle road, this depending on how the individual lives his life is situated central to the circle.

First Nations have communicated in a distinct way, which has become a genetic universal representation of a unique symbolic verbal/nonverbal essence.

This comes from inherent nurturing by a society determined to survive.

Our people are intense in educating their generations to come of who we were and who we are now, the future is by far more important than the magnificence of the self.

Darla Fisher-Odjig   Stanley Fisher   Dominic Odjig
3 Generations

To order additional copies of this book, contact:
Xlibris Corporation
1-888-795-4274
www.Xlibris.com
Orders@Xlibris.com

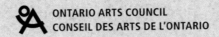

ONTARIO ARTS COUNCIL
CONSEIL DES ARTS DE L'ONTARIO

This book was made possible through an Ontario government agency known as the Ontario Arts Council.

Printed in the United States
By Bookmasters